ON THE BUBBLE

How Being "Othered" Helped Me Grow in My Relationship with Christ and Go Forward in My Relationship With God.

Stephenie L. Hardaway

ISBN: 9798665582856

Printed in the United States of America

This book is dedicated to those who watched me struggle in my effort to write this, to those who encouraged me to complete it and to those who interrupted me along the way.

CONTENTS

INTRODUCTION

◆ ◆ ◆

Being "othered" is something that many have experienced. For some, it pushed them to greatness. For others, it pulled them to destruction. Then there are those like me. We hunger for God's love but live in the misunderstanding that God could never love us. We work all over the church because we have been taught that faith without works is dead. We pray because we have been taught that if we go to God in prayer with a sincere heart, we will be answered. We are given examples of those who have come through whatever we are facing. Yet, nothing changes.

Life becomes theater. We play at being who we think we should be while our hearts hide our truth. It is inevitable that some will give up on God. They will find it impossible to believe that God could love them and walk away. There is a sadness, a finality when you give up on God. There is a hole that no one can fill and it exists until we discover the truth.

The words we have heard to keep us in our place or to move us toward what others think we should be, are often not those of God. There is a love that God has for all of creation that we as humans are unable to fathom. I cannot speak for anyone but myself when I say that the realization that God loves me as me, gave me the courage to walk away from people. I was able to walk away from the boxes that were to not only hold me but to mold me to its shape.

My desire for God was so strong that I walked a walk I knew I was not made to walk. That journey was not mine. My journey may not be believable to some and that's fine. What I am sure of is that I have never been closer to God. There is no one on this earth that can convince me otherwise.

This book was written to help those who are like I was. If you find it heart-wrenching to seek God, you must understand that God sees you. God sees all of you. The topics I chose are some that I had to face in order to move through life. I hope that the insight provided will give hope to those who believe people instead of the still quiet voice within that whispers, "I love YOU."

HOUSEKEEPING

◆ ◆ ◆

Just so we are on the same page, I want to explain the terminology I use for the word, "God."

At times, the word, "Source," appears in place of "God" because it reminds me of the expansiveness of the Creator. It provides a greater understanding of the being that we call our Father, our Creator. The Creator is our Source. There is nothing that I need that Source cannot, will not, or has not already provided.

I understand that some may not be able to see beyond the terminology. For those, I present a challenge. Ask yourself, "Does the word "Source" subtract anything that you know about the one you call God?

When I approach Source, it is with reverence and humility. I understand the Presence and don't take the time that we spend together lightly. My love for Source is nothing compared the love I have been given through Source and Jesus Christ.

Never doubt who I speak of when the word "Source" appears. It is all that is, all that was and all that ever will be.

Stephenie

ON THE BUBBLE

◆ ◆ ◆

When you hear the phrase on the bubble, it is often used when speaking about sports. Some team is on the bubble of being eliminated. It is basically in between success and failure for anything. Lately, I have found myself to be on the bubble when it comes to religion, my faith, my long-held beliefs. Thus, the reason for the title. For years I have wrestled with what I believe, based upon the bible and teaching that I have received.

I was raised in a household with a very active Christian mother. My grandmother was a choir director, my grandfather was a deacon and I was born into that. Unfortunately for them, I was never a kid that you could just tell anything. When I asked a question and the answer was to "just take it on faith," I was less than thrilled with it. I believe that this was the impetus for me stepping outside of Christianity when I got older.

Don't misunderstand. I kept going to church but I studied other religions. I felt that there was something I was not getting. I felt out of the loop. I wanted what others seemed to have. I wanted that close relationship with Jesus. I thought maybe God did not love me because of who I was.

I knew from a young age that I liked girls. I knew that in the bible, it was wrong. I also knew that I was going to hell. I knew it. Yet, I yearned for Jesus to take me away. I prayed for Jesus to "crack the sky open." I felt no kinship with anyone and wanted to leave. A nice way of saying that I wanted to die.

I tried it too. I took a handful of pills thinking that they would take me out. But, surprise! I woke up the next day just fine. I figured that I needed to make some changes in my life. So, I began to work diligently in the church. I became a choir director, a drummer for the choir and I even wrote church plays.

But in my quiet times, I always felt like I was still seeking. I didn't have what everyone else seemed to. I felt attacked in church, which kept me from being honest. One day, I left and have not returned. Not in the traditional sense.

I became part of an organization called, "WHOSOEVER: Community of F.A.I.T.H*- Finding Answers In The Healing. This was the first organization headed by an African-American Pastor who just happens to be a lesbian. I thought, "I found my tribe!" It was an amazing time. She saw something in me that I did not want to admit. She saw the calling. Yet, I was still on the bubble. She gave me the opportunity to speak during service. I still felt lost. I began studying other religions again. But every now and then I would hear a sermon or a speaker that went straight to my issues. Then one day, after the murder of George Floyd, TD Jakes had a conversation with three white pastors, a neuroscientist and an evangelist. They were addressing the white evangelical church's silence on the racial uprising that were happening (and still are at the time of this writing). One of the pastors, Judah Smith, said, "we taught them what to think, we didn't teach them how to think."

"Finally. Finally." I was surprised at my reaction but it was real. I have always felt that church people were really being led instead of being taught. There is more to Jesus than his death. Why was His life not being emphasized as much or more than his death? His life was a perfect guide for us to help us learn how to live with one another. I still do not understand that but what I have come to understand is that I have control of my beliefs. I am actively listening to different conversations, reading different books and focusing on what touches my soul.

This book was written during a time when the country was in the midst of a pandemic and an uprising due to police brutality. We are all on the bubble. The bubbles may be different but they are there. There are issues that we all face that keep us on the bubble. We are near the point of leaving what may mean more to us than anything else. I wanted to take a look at some of the things that keep us on the bubble. They keep us from moving to the next level.

In this book, I explore some of the things that kept me on the bubble. They kept me from fully experiencing the true love of Christ. I now recognize that people fall short of his example and it is up to me to follow it as closely as humanly possible.

MORNINGS WITH SOURCE

◆ ◆ ◆

Every day when I wake up and do my meditation, there's a conversation. It's never about my sexuality unless I make it so. When it is, it's never condemnation. Because my whole objective is to put Source first. I don't see Source through the lens of my sexuality. I used to. I was blinded and bound by it. But the "it" was not Source nor was it my sexuality. The "it" was people. I was too worried about what folks thought and said. It did affect me and my walk with Christ. That was not Source affecting me and my walk with Christ. It was the power that I gave to people. That is, until I came to understand that I owed no man anything except to love him. I owe them that, and only that.

It was then that I was able to go to Source whole and complete. I am not sexually broken. I am who I am. I don't view the world through the lens of what I struggle with but through the lens of who I am in totality. That means that I go to Source open and honestly because Source knows me and there's nothing that I can hide or choose to hide from Source.

So just as there are those who walk through this life struggling, and having made that choice to do that, that's their life. But it's not my life. I don't try to put what I feel on anyone. I just allow Source to use me in the way that I am. Being who I am keeps me and my relationship with Source open and close. I try to walk in the way that Jesus did. However, I am human, not perfect. So, I do make mistakes and therefore, I spend quite a bit of time on the bubble.

Even when I am on the bubble, Source never yells at me. There is never a time when I don't feel secure in the love of Source. Despite my doubts, my fears, my anger at times, I am always resting in the all-encompassing love of Source. There is an ease in our walk together because there is honesty.

I cannot lie to Source. How do you lie to one who knows all that you are? How do you lie to your Creator? Many have tried and failed. The truth is you never lie to Source. You lie to yourself. That's where the damage comes in. We think we are fooling people. What's worse is that we don't even consider the Almighty. We forget that the All-knowing knows all.

Meditation reminds me that I am a part of a being that encompasses the world, the universe. Being that close, is a feeling that I wish all to have. Recognizing that we all are a part and we breathe Source in and breathe Source out. Our exhale is someone else's inhale. We are truly one. That's what makes my mornings with Source incredible.

WHAT IS THE HOLY SPIRIT?

◆ ◆ ◆

Remember the Mentos experiment? Someone would take a bottle of Cola and drop a Mentos into the bottle. As soon as the Mentos hit the cola it would explode out of the bottle. That's how the Holy Spirit is. It is energy within you. The part of the Source that lives within each of us becomes activated by something. Something resonates with Source in us and when it happens, you feel the vibrations. You can feel the tingling in your body. You try to suppress it but the more it is activated, the stronger the vibration. The flow gets so strong that it cannot be contained. It is as the biblical scripture, Jeremiah 20:9 says, "But if I say, "I will not mention his word or speak anymore in his name," his word is in my heart like a fire, a fire shut up in my bones. I am weary of holding it in; indeed, I cannot." You will explode, just as that cola exploded. Just as rocket boosters must reach a certain temperature to cause a rocket to be lifted from a launching pad, it is usually activated by something. Something being said, being heard, or being felt physically. But it touches what's inside of you. That is one manifestation of the Holy Spirit.

The Creator is a divine replicator. We do not have to stand in line to "get" what we already have. It resides within us. We do not have to search for it or beg it to appear. It is always there. According to the bible, Jesus left him with us. The Holy Spirit is our advocate. In John 14, Jesus calls him the "Spirit of Truth." He said, "The world cannot accept him, because it neither sees him nor knows him. But you know him, for he lives with you and will be in you. Did he say that you have to ask for it? No! He (It) was left for us to be with us. No man can give you what God (Source) has already provided.

Don't be afraid to call upon that Spirit. In this life, we all need the Spirit of Truth. Whether Christian or not, there is something within all of us that requires us to be honest. It pushes us past where we thought we could go and comforts us as we walk that road. It will not allow us to lie to ourselves, though we may lie to others.

Soon, we will be unable to do that. Living a lie becomes impossible when we live consciously. When we are aware of the presence of the Holy Spirit, there is no room for deceit. There is only room for growth.

If we continue to develop a relationship, we will grow beyond our expectations. We will be able to walk in a way that we did not think possible. Those who know us will be not believe what they are seeing or who we are becoming. For many, it will be a time of confusion. They may find it impossible to believe that we are the same person that they have always known.

The Holy Spirit is here for all who want it. It is present in each and every person but not everyone is open to that realization. It is truly a gift to those who choose to be open to it. For those who dismiss it, it is my opinion that they are missing something very special. This is what Jesus left for us because He would no longer be a physical presence. No person has ever given me a gift that wonderful and no one can take it from me.

GOD IS LOOKING AT YOU – PSALM 139

◆ ◆ ◆

When you become a member of a church, you become part of a relationship. You pledge your time, talent, and tithes to God and the church. In return the church pledges to love and support you. Source has already done its part. You will find that people who have gone through things and come out on the other side are some of the most faithful people in the church. They show up when others won't, do what is asked of them with little or no complaining, and it's often because of their desperate desire for God. That includes those in the LGBTQ community.

It won't be long before we find out we are not in a reciprocal relationship. As a matter of fact, we are in an abusive relationship. Anyone who is in a relationship, where we are disrespected and beat down for being who we are is in an abusive relationship. I wondered why some in the LGBTQ community would stay in non-affirming churches. There are the usual reasons: family is there, I grew up there, I love the choir, etc. But there has to be more to it. At least in my mind. So, I did some research on why people stay in abusive relationships. A few of them are:

1. Society normalizes unhealthy behavior so people may not understand that their relationship is abusive. Traditional dogma teaches that homosexuality is an abomination. Whole cities were destroyed because of it. This

is being taught as fact. Clobber scriptures pulled from bible are used to clobber people. But this is unhealthy behavior. Calling people out of their name, doing so-called exorcisms, sending kids to conversion therapy is all abusive. Yet, it is not considered abuse because it is done in the name of God and we are considered the worst of the worse.

2. Emotional abuse destroys self-esteem, making it impossible to start fresh. Being told from childhood that you are weird, you need to man up or not walk as hard, act like a girl or don't act like a girl – whatever the words were – they tore you down. The words said when you are in a pew where you are not affirmed can often come at you like a bullet. The longer you stay destroys any self-esteem you may have. Low self-esteem prevents forward motion. You will do whatever you can to please your abuser so that they will say things to lift you up. Even if what you do is lie.
3. Abusive people are great at pretending to be everything you are looking for in a partner and love bomb you with affection. Sound familiar? We love you. We care about you and your soul. After while, the hammer will come down. "You know you would be so pretty with some make-up on. You are such a handsome man. Just buff it up a bit." You start to believe that you ARE the problem. You deserve the abuse because you are not what you are supposed to be in their eyes.

Truth is, no one deserves to be beat down. Can any man guarantee you salvation? The word says, "Whosoever believeth." Being in a welcoming church is great but we need affirmation. Who doesn't want their other half, or loved ones to tell them that they are the best thing going? Don't you want to be told that you mean the world to someone? That's affirmation. When you dedicate yourself to a church that refuses to affirm you, it leaves you empty. If you are not affirmed, you feel not wanted. Not only that but most non-affirming churches refuse to allow you to serve. See you can come, but you cannot do anything unless you change, deny who you are, or remain celibate.

Psalm 39 is clear. There is nowhere that God is not. There isn't anything about us that surprises God. God knitted us together in our mother's wombs. He knows every bone in our body. You can live a lie but you are never lying to God.

The relationship we desire is with God but we end up doing things so that our relationship with man is good. There is nowhere that you can go that God does not know where you are or what you are doing. There is no change in wardrobe or application of make-up that can cover you from God's piercing gaze into your heart. For God already knows you. All of you. Even in the darkness, God sees you. In God's presence is only light. God sees you and still beckons you.

Back in the day when I was struggling, I would watch TBN and an ex-lesbian would pop up every now and then. It would drive me crazy because I have hit my knees many times and asked for change. As have many of my brothers and sisters in the community. We were sincere in our requests but change never happened. Or maybe it did. Maybe the change is not what we asked for but what God wanted. Maybe the change is God showing you your strength to handle people's attitudes towards you. Maybe the change is the disappearance of your self-hatred. Maybe the change is God helping you to recognize your courage to walk out of that abusive situation and into a truly affirming one. Don't be fooled. Be sure that God is watching you.

SHAPESHIFTING

◆ ◆ ◆

Movies about shapeshifters are usually about aliens. But in reality, we are all shapeshifters. We do it all of the time. It is my opinion that we learn how to do it as children. We are being molded into beings that will fit into this world. There are so many things about this world that require certain behavior, we find ourselves being twisted and shoved into places we may not belong. The sad thing is we often do not. The world is full of adults who did not achieve their dreams and when they have children, they see another opportunity to make it happen. These children learn to play the roles that their parents have placed them into. What they forget is that with each passing year, children grow.

When they become adults, some don't even know who they are because it's been all about what others wanted them to be. They enter into friendships and relationships as shapeshifters. They have learned to adjust their behavior to what others want so everything is really false. It can throw them into a tailspin because relationships require compromise. More importantly, they require you to be honest.

How can you be honest when you are busy putting on a performance? The play's the thing, right? There is always an audience. Even in quiet times, the performance is often for one who cannot be fooled. That one is the actor. The actor lives in denial and desires that the lies be true. The heart aches for a truth that is not available.

Some have no idea how to walk into a room as who they truly are. To walk in their truth is unimaginable. What's worse is the day that their shapeshifting affects others. How many have shifted into a marriage just to please others? They become husbands and wives, mothers and fathers, because that is what they are supposed to do. They populate places that would not welcome them in their own skin. It is this knowledge that pushes them further into that world. Until the day that they lose their superpower. They can no longer shapeshift.

They want to, but something inside is now fighting for its life. For its very existence. There is no longer a story that is strong enough to pull them back into line. The audience is now confused. "Who am I looking at?" What happened to you?" Even the shapeshifter is confused. "Who am I?" When on stage, they forget their lines and often slip into a different script. This leaves the other actors confused because they are still in that story. Unfortunately for them, once the shapeshifter leaves the theater, there is no return. That storyline is over and they are now writing their own script.

It is no longer up to the shifter to carry the story. See, the reason for the shifting is to make everyone else comfortable. But when that is no longer a concern, it stops and they begin to write their own story. It is scary but exciting. It is freeing and it is honest. The costume is put away, the lights are turned down and the shifter has left the building.

FORGIVENESS

◆ ◆ ◆

Forgiveness is a loaded word. You will hear those who say forgiveness is for you. It keeps you from holding anger inside. It sets the forgiver free. Then there are those who say that they are done forgiving. They continue to be hurt or betrayed so they feel that forgiveness does nothing. They become bitter. It seems that where the forgiver gets it wrong is in remembering and learning from the lesson. If you continue to trust those who have betrayed or hurt you, then you will continually be hurt. Learn the lesson.

Forgiveness is work. Forgiving those who see nothing wrong with that they have done or continue to do is unbelievable pressure. When we are faced with this type of person, we tend to think of them as doing something to us or making us feel some kind of way. The truth is, they are behaving in a way that may offend us or sometimes cause us pain, but it is always up to us to receive or not receive what they are throwing at us. We must remember that it is our choice to be a trash dump or not. Even if this person is in our household, we do not have to be a receptacle for their foul emissions.

It can seem impossible at times, especially if the offender never views their behavior as offensive or hurtful. They will often portray themselves as the victim. "My father was never there. My mother treated me badly because she hated my father. I was abused." Sometimes the undercurrent of envy flows so deeply that the offender is unaware of its presence. Yet, somehow it makes itself visible to the offended. Perhaps that is the gift that allows the possibility of forgiveness. Being privy to someone else's inner weakness can bring understanding and therefore, forgiveness.

One of the most important things we must recognize in ourselves is the need for peace. The world is noisy enough. We must be able to move through it in a peaceful state. That will not always be the case but it is needed. When there are disrupters in our lives, we can become their victims. The darts that they throw are often dipped in poison. More often than not, their intended victims are not the source of the anger or pain. Those who are hit may have to forgive over and over until they are done. It takes strength to forgive but it takes self-love to remember with peace. Never let your kindness be taken for weakness or your forgiveness for foolishness.

Don't let any person or situation affect your ability to forgive. There is nothing that says you have to return to that situation, but something inside will push you to forgive. Forgiveness may not come immediately, but it is necessary for you to move on. Anger keeps you frozen in place, motionless with the mind recorder set on replay. What many of us fail to realize is that we have control of the recorder.

The recorder in my mind often likes to go into action when I hear something or think about moving to the next level in my writing. Sometimes I will think about ways to get my speaking career off the ground and the recorder will click on just to remind me of a horrible situation I found myself in the time I decided to take a chance. It's like a little saboteur.

What I find myself doing during these times is talking to the recorder. Yep, I treat it like the saboteur it is at that time. It has no business disrupting my now by bringing up my then. Only after I address it will the recorder move on. And I forgive myself because the recorder is part of me.

VISION

◆ ◆ ◆

Proverbs 29:18 says, "Where there is no vision, the people perish: but he that keepeth the law, happy is he." (KJV) The NIV version says: "Where there is no revelation, the people cast off restraint; But happy is he who keeps the law." The Message translation says, "If people can't see what God is doing, they stumble all over themselves; But when they attend to what He reveals, they are most blessed."

I must confess when I first learned this scripture, I learned the King James version. I quickly learned what it meant or what I thought it meant. As I read different translations, I found that I was a bit short in my understanding. My understanding of the word "perish" was that it meant "to die."

But it simply means to be unrestrained, to be scattered as in all over the place.

When I think about Source, I have a vision of what that is. In my mind, it is creative energy, loving energy, compassionate energy. But what if it is just energy? Energy that when flowing through a certain conduit causes things to happen? Like plugging something into a wall socket that is plugged into an energy source.

We all want what I call Source and others call God, the Universe, etc. to be what we envision. Of course, the marginalized want a loving, compassionate and just God. Otherwise, we could not survive. Suicide rates would be much higher than they are now.

Those who claim to be pro-lifers, who are abstinent, who are bible literalists, want their God to fulfill their vision. They want a God that rages at sin as they do. They want that angry God that Calvin preached about.

That's what vision is. It's not physical sight, but thought and faith about what we believe to be true.

What is your vision of yourself? That is the question.

If you don't believe in something, you'll fall for anything. That scripture means that if you don't have faith in something, you will be all over the place. Where is your faith? During the storm Jesus slept. When they woke him, he spoke and the winds calmed and the waters stilled. Then he turned to them and asked, "Where is your faith?" They had seen and still their belief, their faith was shaky. Where there is no vision, the people perish.

Where is your faith? What is your vision? When you have no vision for your life, you perish. You will be all over the place because you have no anchor. Your faith, your vision anchors you.

CORONA

◆ ◆ ◆

As you all know, the Coronavirus has moved all over the world and has infected millions at the time of this writing. Covid-19 has proven to be elusive in the search for a cure or vaccine for that matter. During this time, many find themselves out of work and even out of business. I am one of the fortunate "essential" employees. However, I talk to those who have to deal with this every day. Hearing the initial uncertainty in their voices and later the frustration begins to weigh on me. I understand. I have been out of work. I have had to swallow my pride and depend on others. Yet, it was not illness or a new virus that changed my world. It was a decision made by someone else or even a choice I made. So, being in this new world has caused all of us to look at our worlds in a different way.

Today, I heard that a 15-year-old girl took her life because she could not deal with being separated from her friends. We have needs that we take for granted. We need human touch and for so many who have family in different parts of the country, this time is very difficult. To not be able to hug my mother, was not something I thought I would experience. At least while both of us are still above ground. I can understand the emotional struggle. To assist with maintaining my sanity, I meditate.

So, as I was meditating, a question popped into my mind: "What is Corona?" I looked it up and found that one definition of Corona is "the rarefied gaseous envelope of the sun and other stars. The amazing thing is that you can only see it during a full eclipse of the sun. I started wondering, spiritually what does that mean? Honestly, when I really started thinking about it, and I had to think about it a few days because you know, sometimes the first thing that comes to your mind, you can't understand it. It can be a little too deep. You have to go back and visit it. I went back to visit it and it kept coming to me. It kept coming to me. Then one day, it finally popped into my brain that a full eclipse darkens the sun. It covers the sun which is the light. When I looked at that I said, "Well, America was in a dark place. America is in a dark place and many of us felt like we couldn't see the light. We felt like the light was being overshadowed by the leader of the free world, overshadowed by the frequency of lies that it almost has become normal. The villainization of journalism and journalists who were doing their jobs correctly. The uplifting of fake news. The ability of news personalities to tell lies, pass them off as truth and people accepted it. Yet, they want to blame the problems of America on certain groups of people.

Instead of looking at what they are actually believing, who they voted in and because America went that way, the world followed. The world grew darker because it was okay to hate. It was okay to kill people based upon hate. It was okay for 45 to call people "sons of bitches" and countries "shithole" countries because he preferred immigrants of a lighter hue. Oh, it's okay for the leader of the free world to say he wants Norwegian immigrants. Yes, it's okay to love who you are. Don't get me wrong. Have pride in who you are because I do. I am proud of who I am. I am also realistic in seeing that you don't have to villainize another group of people to be okay with who you are. And that's what was going on.

Children in cages. Labelling every brown immigrant as a rapist and a drug dealer. The world grew darker. As the world grew darker, so did our souls. Many of our souls grew darker because we wanted a supreme court that believe what we believe and would put into place what we wanted. So, we accepted the lowest of the low, we accepted dirt, we accepted filth, we accepted people who have no business being in the highest court in the land. We accepted someone that led us into the darkness.

Enter Covid-19, the coronavirus. In the middle of the best year, never had lower unemployment, stock markets doing better than they ever had and then...the coronavirus. The light around the darkness. What is a virus? A virus is an invader, an infector that requires a host. When I tell you that this thing is invading, it is invading. It is making people stand up and take notice. But there are still a lot of unbelievers because they are watching and listening to people who are lying. Yet, here we are. Here we are. The light around the darkness.

Keep your eyes on the light. There is no better place to see the light shine than in the darkness. Because that light around the darkness is the sun and the sun will shine again. That's all you have to believe in. Even though its dark, the sun still shines. You can see it. You can see it around this darkness if you just look. Just look.

HERE

◆ ◆ ◆

As I walked along the path to the river, I asked Source, "Where are you?" In that moment I heard the water crash against the rocks as it overflowed its banks. I stood in wonder for a bit, then started to walk. I kept walking and asked again, "Where ARE you?" Just then I felt the wind blow past my body lightly kissing my face. I raised my hand to touch my face but stopped out of habit. I began walking and asked earnestly, "Where are YOU?" I heard the rustle of the leaves in the trees that hang over my head. I looked up expectantly but was drawn back by the feeling of someone watching me. I saw no one. I continued my stroll. I asked once again, "WHERE ARE YOU?" In the silence, I heard "Here."

The second I heard the word, "here" I felt energy flow from my body. I watched it take leaves from the trees and water from the river. It held them in the wind which blended them together. It poured into me the River of Life. It poured wisdom, compassion, love, peace, joy and hope. All that I needed was poured into me. Then energy flowed back into me.

It was then that I realized that it had taken Source and poured it into me. It had taken God and poured it into me. As I walked on, I felt the question rise in me. But before it could come out, I heard my voice say, "HERE."

ACKNOWLEDGEMENT

I want to start by acknowledging the creative force behind everything I do: Source. Without this Presence, life is unbearable. I would not know how to move forward, or move at all. Life is such an adventure. The adventure has been made grander with the knowledge that the most High walks, runs and climbs with me on every journey I take.

I also want to acknowledge those who have played a role in what I am now doing. My wife Sharlene has watched my struggles and been there through the good and the bad. She has watched my spiritual growth as well as supported me in it. My mother, Bobbie Jackson, who has given me such support when many have turned their backs on their children. She shows what many only speak: the love of Jesus. My friend and co-host, Starla Carr, who has walked this journey with me. We have hosted our podcast for the past six years. Your mind never ceases to amaze me and your talent will soon light up the world .

Finally, I would like to thank Pastor Dionne Boyice of WHOSOEVER: Community of F.A.I.T.H. Thank you for each opportunity that you gove me to hone my speaking skills. But more than that, you gave me the opportunity to present the Jesus that I know. For that, I will forever be grateful.

ABOUT THE AUTHOR

Stephenie L. Hardaway

Stephenie L. Hardaway is a published author, inspirational speaker and co-host of the podcast "We Said That!" She has been married for six years, has two children and a granddaughter.

BOOKS BY THIS AUTHOR

The Round-Up

Former FBI agents Haley Akers and Robin Barnes are investigating missing LGBTQ activists. During the investigation, Haley disappears, which leaves Robin to question her superiors' actions. Meanwhile, Haley's girlfriend Jai has joined a squad of former soldiers to look for the missing. Will Jai find her best friend? What will she do when she discovers Haley is now missing as well?

www.ingramcontent.com/pod-product-compliance
Lightning Source LLC
LaVergne TN
LVHW050349160826
845677LV00019BA/2809

* 9 7 9 8 6 6 5 5 8 2 8 5 6 *